Lights!
Camera!
YOU!

Lights!
Camera!
YOU!

A Practical Guide for Creating and Using Video to Market Your Practice

Laura J Nadler

ISBN 978-1-7370098-0-1

Cover and interior photos | Shutterstock
Screenshots | Laura J Nadler
Cover design | Laura J Nadler
Author photo | Jason H Nadler

Printed in The United States of America

Published by WorkingCat, Inc.

Visit **www.workingcat.pro**

For Jason

My Benedick. My Clyde. My F. Scott.
Thank you.

Table of Contents

Introduction

Thank you purchasing this book! It may seem small, but it is chock full of useful, real-world information for creating and using video to market your dental practice.

When I first started coaching and training dental practices on marketing it seemed there was a new platform every day. Some lasted (Facebook), some didn't (MySpace, Vine, Google+) and some just leapt to the front of the pack (Instagram). Through all of these, the one constant that I've seen is that practices are willing to try platforms they use in their real lives, like Facebook and Instagram, but as soon as I say, "Let's make some videos and put them on YouTube!" they start looking at their shoes and hoping I change the subject or go away.

I get it. Video is outside the comfort zone of most people, and from the outside it can seem incredibly complicated. I wrote this book because I found that once I worked with a practice to get their videos done, they were so much more comfortable that I would start seeing fresh new video popping up in their marketing all the time. That's my goal: to take the scary out of the process so you can jump in and create video to share your amazing story with the world—or at the very least, with future patients.

There are two main sections of the book:

Creating Your Videos

I will take you through all the prep and process of creating engaging videos and even talk about how to hire a pro—if you choose that route. I recommend you read ALL of Part 1 before you start making your videos. I've done my best to answer all the questions that I know come up along the way. Then you can go back to individual sections for reference as you're creating your videos.

I have also created a special resources page on my website just for you – yes, you! It's full of example videos, templates, and checklists to guide you on your journey.

The secret page is **www.workingcat.pro/videoresources**.

Using Your Videos

I'll discuss the places you should use your videos, the different formats each platform prefers and all the background tools to make sure you get found online. I will get pretty granular on the YouTube process and include a whole lot of screen shots so even a novice will be able to make the most of your videos.

Each section contains multiple chapters and headings to make sure you have all the tools and information you need to be successful. There are checklists for preparing and Pro Tips to help you along the way.

Do I Really Need Video?

Since you're here, you must know it's time to add video to your marketing mix. But maybe some folks on the team (I might even be looking at you, Doc) think this is a waste of time. If I had a nickel for every time someone asked me, "Do I really need to do video?"...well...I'd have a lot of nickels.

The short answer is yes, you do, and I'm here to give you some very compelling reasons why. These aren't just my opinions; this is data from folks who know their stuff.

- Video sparks interest. About 46% of people say they'd be more likely to seek out info about a service after seeing it in an online video. (Source: Eloqua)
- Video improves your ranking. Having a video on the landing page of your site makes it 53% more likely to show up on page 1 of Google SEO. (Source: Mist Media)
- Video keeps them on your site longer. The average user spends 88% more time on a website with video. (Source: Mist Media)

And according to Bitable's *55 Video Marketing Statistics*

- 55 % of internet users watch online videos every day.
- 90 % of consumers say video helped them make a purchasing decision.

- Videos on social media generate 1200% more shares than images and texts.
- Including video in your Dental Marketing strategy can increase your web traffic by over 41 percent.

Video—especially on YouTube and social platforms like Instagram and Facebook—is gaining in popularity almost daily. In fact, YouTube is the 2nd most popular search engine in North America—sorry Bing!

Despite all the awards and accolades for content from Netflix and Amazon, YouTube still has significantly more users. That means more opportunities for you to be seen.

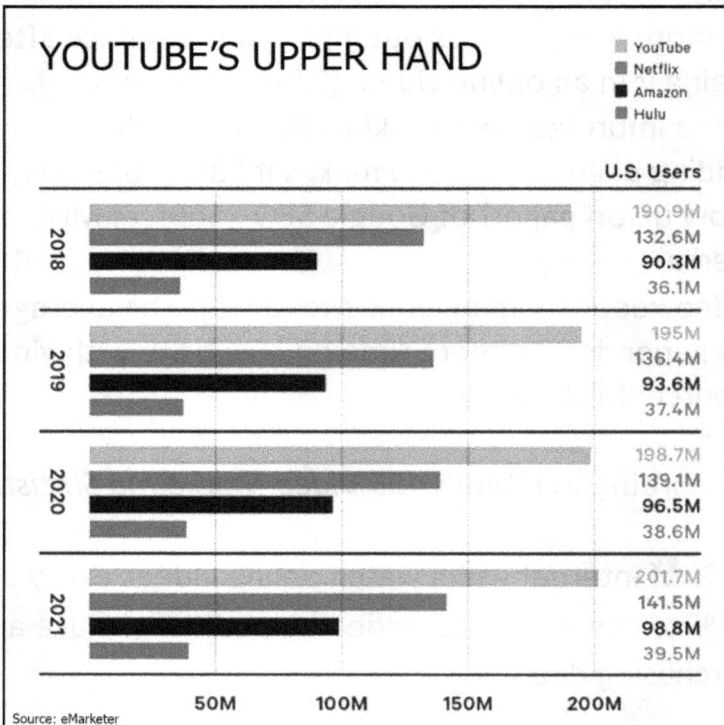

YOUTUBE'S UPPER HAND

- YouTube
- Netflix
- Amazon
- Hulu

U.S. Users

Year	YouTube	Netflix	Amazon	Hulu
2018	190.9M	132.6M	90.3M	36.1M
2019	195M	136.4M	93.6M	37.4M
2020	198.7M	139.1M	96.5M	38.6M
2021	201.7M	141.5M	98.8M	39.5M

50M   100M   150M   200M

Source: eMarketer

Will 200 million people see your videos? No. But like the lottery, you've got to be in it to win it. Unlike the lottery, video marketing guarantees exposure and return.

I know numbers like that can make this sound like a daunting prospect, but I promise, I'm going to make this manageable and—as we like to say here in Dental World—painless.

Let's Go!

Part 1

Creating Your Videos

Where do I start?

First, let's talk about mindset. To create engaging videos that truly tell your story, we need an engaged team that is willing to have a bit of fun. Have a team meeting first to talk about your desire (need) to get this started. Get feedback, from ideas to concerns, and really listen and respond to that feedback. The team should feel they have a voice in the process, especially because we need their A-Game on shoot day.

Let the team know that once you create all your amazing content which we'll cover here in Part 1, you will still need to put it to good—and frequent—use. We'll cover all of that in Part 2.

Once we have buy-in from the team, let's look at planning out your videos. I tell my clients to create 24 videos in the first year.

I know. I just lost you. 24!?!?! Are you crazy, woman!?!?

Just wait until you see how fast we can get to 24.

Chapter 1 | The Big Ones First

The videos we're going to cover first require the most planning and effort.

These are your "evergreen" videos. They will always be there—on YouTube, your website, etc. It pays to spend some time—and maybe money—on these since they will be a calling card for your brand and practice. You may choose to update them over the years, but generally these themes will stay with you.

This is the list of "must have" videos for marketing your practice. If you never do any others, do these:

Evergreen Videos

- Meet the Doc
- Meet the Team
- Patient Testimonials
- Your Top 5 Services
- 5 Post Op Instructions
- Office Tour
- Hero Video

That's already 15 of the 24 even if you only have one doc and a small team. If you have more docs or a bigger team, you could be approaching 20!

I will cover what goes into each of these separately. We'll add more as we go that are specific to events, holidays, and your goals. We'll talk later about these one-off and on-the-fly videos in **Chapter 7 - "Keep it Fresh!"**

What exactly are these Evergreen Videos?

I will show you exactly how to create each of these a bit later. In this section I want you to understand what a finished version of each will contain and how it will flow, so don't worry (yet) about the minutia like types of images and the voice-overs. I promise—I've got you! Your "Meet the" videos will be the most watched. They need to tell your story clearly and represent you and your practice in the most authentic way.

Meet the Doc

Each Doctor in the practice should have their own video. This video should include the Doctor talking about what inspired them to become a dentist, why they love it and a bit about them outside the office—skydiving, gourmet cook, animal lover, etc.

It should include sections with them speaking directly to the camera and sections where their voice is heard over footage of them interacting with patients and the team.

Meet the Team

It may surprise you to know that after the home page, the most frequently clicked-on page on a dental website is "Meet the Team"—sorry, Doc! Patients want to know who you are, and these videos are a great way to show them.

These should include each team member introducing themselves, and some images of them interacting with patients and the rest of the team.

Sometimes you'll need more than one of these depending on the size of your team. For example, you can split the Clinical and Admin teams into two separate videos, or divide up Assistant, Hygiene and Admin for three. If your team is HUGE, you can do as one of my clients did and only feature your team leads in the **To-Camera** bits while including a bit of everyone in the **B-Roll**.

I'll give you more on that in the how-to's for each video type in **Chapter 3**, under **"To-Who? B-What?"**

Patient Testimonials

The best patient testimonial videos each feature 2-3 patients in one, but if you've got patients lining up to sing your praises, you can certainly make more than one of these.

We want to feature images of them telling us why they love the practice and sections of their voice over footage of them approaching the front desk, talking to the RDH in the dental chair, in the Doc's office for a consult, etc.

Your Top 5 Services

By top services I mean the ones you love doing that also make you money: veneers, whitening, implants, Invisalign, etc.

These videos will be almost entirely voice-over as we show patients what we do best. It can feature images of the Doc referencing X-rays or a model. It should feature smiling patients. Talking about same day crowns? Show your CEREC doing its magic!

Most importantly this does not need to be—nor should it be—just you talking to the camera. Videos work for a reason. We retain so much more when we're shown something than when we're told about it, so make sure to show.

5 Post Op Instructions

For "Post Ops" think extraction, implant, whitening, endo, crown & bridge, bridge & tunnel (⊘NY-er joke!)

These are always most effective when the person who explains them in the office does it in the video—for a couple of reasons. These people are most used to doing it and will sound more comfortable. When a patient hears it repeated in the same way, it's more likely to sink in.

Again, these don't all have to be to-camera. A perfect example is how to load your take-home whitening trays. Usually, a Dental Assistant or Hygienist does this in office. Have that person in the video and when they get to the meat of the process, move your filming down to focus on their hands—the part of them actually showing how.

Office Tour

This can be a quick walk through of the practice highlighting the things that set you apart—like that espresso maker or those hot towels. It's also a great place to show off technology like that cone beam CT or your new filtration system.

Generally, these are best narrated by a member of the team. Consider splitting the job with your OM covering the front and your DA covering the back.

Hero Video

You've seen these. They usually appear as the banner image on a website. They are generally silent, but some have music. It's simply a series of images of the team, patients, office, etc. that give the vibe of your practice. It typically does not include any direct speaking. We'll talk later about other ways to use them too.

Chapter 2 | Preparation!!!
It saves a lot of perspiration later.

I know that shooting video for most people is the single most uncomfortable part of their marketing process. We may use Instagram and Facebook in our real lives but sitting in front of a camera talking about ourselves is generally not what we do day to day. So how do we make this painless for everyone involved?

First, start planning well before the day you plan to record (or shoot). These Evergreen videos shouldn't be spur of the moment. You have decisions to make, lists to prepare, and people to invite (for those testimonials), so when you finish reading and decide to get started, allow at least a week or two before the big day.

There are 7 key steps to preparing to shoot your main, evergreen videos:

1. **Appoint a Producer.**

   Think of this person as the boss for the process.

They will finalize the **Shot List** (see #3) and lay out the timeline of the day based on that. That list tells you who needs to be where and when. They will oversee the filming to ensure all the footage on the Shot List is captured. They can be the person who asks the interview questions. They will also make sure footage is being backed up as noted in **Chapter 4** under **"Here We Go!"**

The Producer should not be the camera person. They each have enough to think about.

2. **Decide on the tone of your videos.**

   Your videos should represent your brand and the reality of your practice. Seeing a video of a super-intense, stuffy Pedo office will feel off-putting to parents and kids. But if you are a serious, buttoned down practice, don't be all goofy for the camera. It will be jarring to patients to learn that's not the vibe in your practice when they arrive.

   It's a good idea to look at other practice videos and select a few that you think best mesh with your brand and style. You can see some examples on that special resources page I mentioned earlier.

3. **Decide on the footage you want to capture and create a Shot List.**

You don't want to do all this work and realize you forgot someone. This also makes it easier to manage the day because everyone knows where they need to be and when.

A **checklist** that covers the main shots every practice must have is on that resources page—download that puppy. Remember it's a starting point. Your practice is unique, and your videos need to tell YOUR story, so add to this list to make sure your videos tell the best version of that story.

4. **Decide on your best locations to film.**

   Not all places are lit well, so take some test videos to see where people look best. Avoid harsh overhead light or direct sunlight. Neither is flattering and both create dark shadows. Beware of fluorescents—they can make things look green on video. NOT a good look.

5. **Make sure all team members have well thought-out answers to those key questions.**

   You'll find these in **Chapter Three** and on the online resources page.

   Again, not scripted, but reviewed so it flows naturally.

6. **Set aside a day to capture all of the footage when the only patients in the office are the testimonials.**

    Trust me—you want a day. And trying to juggle patients will make this a burden on everyone, which will make no one want to do it. I know this one is hard for a lot of docs to swallow, but it's an investment in your practice—just like going to a course. Make it count.

7. **Have everyone watch the videos you selected in step 2.**

    This helps everyone see what you're looking to achieve. It also shows them that other practices do this: none of them are professionals, but they still look great.

Decisions, Decisions

Who will be filming?

One person? Everybody?

Though getting everyone as involved as possible can seem like a good idea, I would limit the role of videographer to ONE or TWO people. Not everyone will be comfortable with the technology, and shoot day is no time to be learning how to use equipment. Speaking of equipment...

Will you be using a video camera, dSLR camera, point and shoot with video function, or a phone?

There are pros and cons to each, but the single most important factor is the comfort level of the operator. If you've got a phone with a high-quality lens—like that iPhone version bazillion—there is no reason to go out and buy expensive equipment.

Talk to the team. You might be surprised to learn that one of them (or one of their kids!) is an excellent photographer/videographer with a great camera. This could be a fun opportunity for them to showcase their skills!

Chapter 3 | Capture Your Footage

Meet the Doc and Team videos

The best "Meet the" videos feature a mix of To-Camera and B-Roll footage. So what does that mean?

To-Who? B-What?

To-Camera footage is the subject (doc/team) telling their story to the camera.
The easiest way to accomplish this is by answering these questions with your own story:

> Who am I? – Your name
> What do I do? – Your role in the practice
> What made me want to do it? – As a child I had a great dentist.
> Why do I love it? – Happy smiles give me joy!

You won't actually ask the questions *on* camera. That would be boring to viewers and eat up precious seconds in your final videos. You will ask them from *behind* the camera.

These prompts make the subject more comfortable, and their responses will always sound more natural than if we just tell them to recite their answers.

Everyone should think about their answers before filming starts, but DO NOT script it. Viewers can spot script reading a mile away. It never sounds genuine. Since the purpose of this is to give prospective patients a feel for you and the practice, you want to be as YOU as possible. If you're usually very serious, don't feel the need to joke around, but if you're usually funny and lighthearted—be that! Patients choose providers base on the person they are—not the degree on the wall.

You Do You: Wear what you wear!
Practice in scrubs? Then film in scrubs. I
want to see the actual people I'm going to
meet in the practice. **(Pro Tip)**

B-Roll. That's just the pro term for what I like to call the "action shots". This is the doc and the team doing what they do best—talking to patients, reviewing a case, having a meeting, etc.

These are not done *to-camera* but caught in a more candid style—even if it is staged. You can sit around your conference table or in an op and pretend you're doing these things. They should look like someone just happened to catch you explaining treatment to a patient, or the team having a laugh.

B-Roll footage is used so the finished video isn't just 90-120 seconds of a person talking to the camera. It's hard to hold a viewer's attention for that long—we're not all George Clooney!

This combination of To-Camera and B-Roll creates a visually pleasing story that will hold the viewer's attention—which is the whole goal.

If a professional video company captures your footage, then editing all these bits together should be part of the package. More on that in **Chapter 6, "Is it Time to Go Pro?",** but you can do it yourself using any number of different programs out there. We'll look at this later in **Chapter 7, "The Cutting Room Floor".**

Patient Testimonials

Use the To-Camera plus B-Roll approach for these as well.

For the B-Roll, show them entering the practice, being greeted at the front desk and talking with the doc in the operatory or consult room.

The voice over will unify all the footage. Knowing that it's not going to be wall-to-wall them on camera will also make it easier on the patient, so show them examples.

The To-Camera footage will be them answering questions.

Questions for the patients:

How long have you been coming to the practice?
What made you choose us?
What do you like most about the practice?

If the patient has had a particularly transformative experience in your practice (full mouth reconstruction, getting past the fear of dentists, beautiful new smile) ask them if they'd be willing to talk about that. If so, also get their OK to splice in a before image of their case.

Remember to get a model release signed by any patient you film. There is a model release template available on the resources page that you can customize with your brand logo and practice info, like this:

WorkingCat
a Marketing & Consulting firm

Model Photo/Video Release Form

I, (Patient Name), hereby authorize (Practice Name) or any of their assignees to take photographs, slides, and/or videos of my teeth, jaws, and face. I understand that the photographs, slides, and/or videos will be used as a record of my care, and may be used for communication with other health care professionals, educational publications (dental journals), and educational lectures.

The content may also be used for marketing purposes (including website publication, social media posts, etc). I further understand that if the photographs, slides, and/or videos are used in any publication or as a part of a demonstration, my identifying information (first name only) could be used unless stated differently below. I waive ownership of all photographs, slides, and/or videos.

I do not expect compensation, financial or otherwise, for the use of these photographs. If I wish to revoke this consent, I may do so in writing.

Please initial one option:

_____I do not mind if my photographs/videos are used in any of the above stated situations.

_____I only agree to have my teeth shown without any identifying features.

Signed_____Date_____

Post Op and Top Services

Some of the best versions of Top Services videos include a quick To-Camera intro: "Today we're going to show you how we do same day crowns", followed by mostly B-Roll of the process with voice-over. You may find it easier to record the B-Roll, edit it together, and then add the voice as though you are narrating the process. MANY YouTube pros do this in their instructional videos. Chef John of FoodWishes.com is a great example of this!

For things like veneers and implants, splice in images of your cases or animations of the procedure. You can find these animations all over the internet, and your preferred vendor likely has some you can use—ask your rep! About those images...

NO JUICY PICS!

That means no retracted, saliva-filled, handpiece-in-the-mouth images. This isn't a presentation to your peers and colleagues—it's a marketing video to get people to come in and have these services performed by YOU. Don't freak them out!

Office Tour

These should start either outside the building, so we see signage, or if you're in a larger shared building, outside the door with your practice name.

The point is to take a prospective patient through their journey in your office. Enter and pan around the reception area, stop at the front desk, walk into the back, highlight any awesome tech.

Like your Top Services videos, add narration later so it's clearer and you don't have to start filming again if someone misspeaks.

Hero Video

This is a 30 second video made up entirely of B-roll footage. It can have music if that suits your practice and brand. The best thing about it is you don't need to capture any special footage since you'll have it all from your other videos—woohoo!

A Hero Video is generally used in a loop as the home page banner on your website, but with some voice-over audio it can become the Channel Trailer for your YouTube Channel. We'll cover that in the chapter on **Advanced Stuff** in **Part 2.** You can also use this version if you advertise on YouTube, or as an actual TV commercial. Remember those?

Chapter 4 | Ready for My Close-Up

The Day Before the Shoot

Put all that stuff away! You know what I mean—**The Stuff**.

We know it's a dental practice, but we don't need all the *Stuff of Dentistry* out on the counters. Jars of 2x2's, carpules, swabs and such should all be tucked away. They show up as clutter on screen (even in your still photos!), so find them new homes for the day.

Same goes for brochures and stacks of magazines in the reception area and charts out on the front desk. Yes, it's fake clean, but trust me, you will be so much happier with the end result. Who knows—it might even inspire you edit permanently.

Do NOT leave this for the morning of the shoot. You don't want that kind of pressure.

It's Shoot Day!!

Breathe. You've prepared for this! The key for today is to keep it upbeat and light. Pressure and negativity will show in the finished product.

Anytime we do something outside our comfort zone it takes more of our concentration and wears us out faster than our normal day. Make sure to schedule breaks and lunch. A post-shoot team party never hurt either!

Here we go!

- First thing: The Producer reviews the Shot List with everyone and makes sure to answer any lingering questions.
- Turn off things that make noise: suction, phones, background music, TV's. Your camera mic will pick these up and they will be distracting. The background noise will take away from your final videos.
- Film each person's To-camera footage first. Better to capture this when everyone is FRESH! And remember, if it's not your turn in front of the camera—**Quiet on the set!**
- Hit record and **take a beat** before speaking. Better to edit out a few seconds of quiet than miss a word if the recording hasn't quite started.
- Try to remember to take a breath between sentences. Those little gaps make editing easier and

small pauses make your videos more pleasurable for the viewer.

- People will make mistakes. That's the beauty of digital filming. Mispronounced your own name? No worries—just start over!

Take 2! It's a good idea to get more than one take of people's answers so you can choose the best versions when you edit.
(Pro Tip)

- Capture B-roll footage next. Be aware of not crowding the frame with too many people when showing interaction. It can make your office look small. Even if it is tiny, we don't want to brag about it. But do get a shot of the whole gang, either out front or in reception.
- Get some shots of the outside of your building (if appropriate) and the entrance to the practice. It's good to grab these toward the end of the day because outdoor footage captured in "The Golden Hour"—the hour before sunset—is beautiful and very welcoming.
- If you're filming on a phone, make sure to periodically upload the footage to another device

or cloud-based server. Nothing is worse than losing all that work.

- If you're shooting with an actual camera, make sure you have enough memory cards and back them up to another device or the cloud throughout the day as well.

Like the movies! When recording on a phone for YouTube, Facebook or your website hold the phone horizontally—like your TV—to avoid those weird fuzzy bands on the sides. (Pro Tip)

Did you get everyone? Did everyone survive? See, I told you this would be painless.

Now go have that party. We'll cover editing next but don't rush into it. For most teams I work with, this was the hard part. Most anyone can learn to use editing software but being on camera comes naturally to very few. Congratulations on being awesome!

You did it!

Chapter 5 | The Cutting Room Floor

You have shot way more video than you will keep in the finished product, so get ready to edit.

There are all kinds of video editing software out there from iPhone apps to full-on Adobe editing suites. Your budget, time, experience, and preferences will determine which you use. There are books (and videos!) devoted to teaching only editing, and tons of easy-to use software that will give you professional results. Chances are someone on your staff—or their amazing kid—is a wiz.

Because of that variety I will not cover the specific details of editing software, but I will give you guidelines for editing your footage that will apply no matter which one you use.

These tips will ensure that your finished videos are appealing, professional, and most importantly, they tell your unique story. Take a look at that resources page again and watch those videos to see examples of these tips in action.

- First thing—make a back-up copy of all your footage. Then if anything goes sideways during editing you still have all the raw footage. Work on the copy.
- Keep finished videos between 90 and 120 seconds—less for some post ops and services. Data shows a MASSIVE drop off in viewer retention around that 2-minute mark.
- Be sure to open with your brand logo and practice name. This can be a shot of your signage, a title card, or a text overlay like this:

- Add titles to "Meet the" videos. If your Dental Assistant is saying, "Hi, I'm Chris and I'm a Certified Dental Assistant", that should appear on screen in a text overlay.

- The individual intro-shot should always be to-camera. Don't cut away to B-roll until they introduce themselves.
- The audio from their answers should continue over the B-roll. You can certainly edit or shorten this to capture the best versions of what they said.
- Watch for changes to wardrobe and lighting between takes, especially if you have takes from multiple days.
- You want to make sure that transitions from image to image are smooth—no choppy transitions. The software can do this for you, use one second fades or two second swipe transitions as your software allows.
- Always include a call to action at the end. "We'd love to meet you." "Call us for an appointment." These look great included in the end title card with your practice name, phone number and website.

WorkingCat
a Marketing & Consulting firm

Online Marketing Course
From Found to Five Stars
Market Your Dental Practice Like You Mean It!

Eligible for 6 CEU's

Learn more at www.workingcat.pro

- Think about adding a bit of music to the intro and end credit. There are all kinds of stock music out there for this purpose—often right in the editing software. Be sure not to use licensed music. You may love that artist, but you don't want to get a cease-and-desist letter for "borrowing" their tunes.
- Life is full of meetings and partings. Don't panic about team members who may leave or new ones who join. They can always be edited in or out as needed. We did this for a client recently, and you'd never know we touched their video.

Don't forget to hang on to all your raw footage. In **Part 2** we'll talk about repurposing content so having a cache of your awesomeness will come in handy. It will also make minor team or technology changes easier to address.

Chapter 6 | Is It Time to Go Pro?

Yes, a GoPro is a type of camera, but what I'm talking about here is spending some money and having a professional shoot and edit your Evergreen videos. As I've said, these are going to be around for a while and will be a representation of your brand and practice, so if the plan I've laid out seems like just too much for you and the team, then it's time to consider hiring a pro.

Many of my clients have chosen this option for their Evergreens, and then go on to shoot their social media and one-off videos themselves. It certainly results in a polished, professional look. One of the biggest things I hear after a pro shoot is how comfortable and easy the videographer made it for the practice. It helps everyone get used to being filmed so those smaller ones will seem less scary.

No matter which pro you choose, expect them to use a full day in the practice (or possible other locations) and to capture a few hours of raw footage to be edited into your final videos.

About that editing...

Probably the single biggest advantage to hiring a pro is having all the editing work done for you. Even if being fabulous on camera comes naturally to you and the team, editing can be daunting. And although it CAN be done by you, I would hate to see you shoot all this great footage and then have it sit there. So be honest with yourself about how much you want to do and your skill level in doing it. There is no shame in outsourcing these big ones. Most of my clients do.

Although you will still be involved in planning and choosing what you want filmed, a lot of that should be taken care of by your pro, typically through questionnaires and/or calls that establish the goals and timeline for the big day.

This is How We Do It.

When our video production team at WorkingCat works with a practice, we have a pre-shoot call with you, me, and our producer to discuss your wants and goals. We send questionnaires to the practice to learn about you and what you want to cover. We create that all important Shot List and schedule for the day. We also edit all the raw footage into complete time-appropriate videos including titles, overlays and music. We ask you to review those videos and request any changes you want before we go to final production.

---

6 Things You Should Ask Before Hiring a Pro:

1. <u>Will you bring additional lighting and equipment?</u> You want a yes to that.
2. <u>Who owns the finished videos?</u> They should belong to the practice.
3. <u>Can I see some of your previous work *with dentists*?</u> Yes, please! Just because they produced a great restaurant video does not mean they can capture a great dental video. Our industry is so different and having someone who's been in it is important.
4. <u>Are your fees all-inclusive, or will I need to pay for edits, titles, music, etc</u>? You want one up-front fee for all—no surprises!
5. <u>How many finished videos do you get for the price</u>? This will vary based on your needs, the company you choose, and what you're spending, but it should be spelled out in the agreement. Again—no surprises! To be truly transparent, expect to spend in the thousands—*not 10's of thousands*, but not 1 or 2 either. As of 2021 most of our clients fall in the $5000-$7000 range depending on the size of the team and number of doctors.
6. <u>How long will it take to get my final videos?</u> With our team, you should expect to see the first edits of your videos in 2-3 weeks, followed by another week or two for any edits you request. Just make sure you get a firm answer from your pro. "Soon" and "Quickly" are not answers.

Shoot Day with a Professional

The pro will run the shoot based on the shot list and schedule—no need to appoint a Producer. That said, appoint someone on your team who knows the players to help in people wrangling, and making sure the videographer knows where everything is.

Make sure the pro is scheduled to arrive early so they can look around the office for the best backgrounds and set up lighting as needed.

If you realize that you didn't include something in the Shot List that you absolutely want to capture, tell them up front—don't wait for the end. They will surely make the adjustment, but it's easier for everyone to work it into the flow of the day from the start.

In that same vein, if there are areas you don't want them to capture (is the lab just a sight?) let them know. It's better than having to edit it out later.

"Feed Me Seymour! Every one of my clients includes the videographer in their lunch order. Nobody likes a hungry artist who's responsible for making you look fabulous!"
☺ *(Pro Tip)*

So that's all your evergreen videos in the can—woohooo! Nice work!

Take a breather for at least a week and then let's look at other, less formal videos you should make throughout the year.

Chapter 7 | Keep It Fresh!

If you've already finished your evergreen videos—and didn't skip ahead like naughty little monkeys—then you have done the very hardest part. Everything from here on out will seem like a picnic.

The videos in this chapter will be less produced and easier to manage. Sometimes only one or two people need to be involved.

There will be two types of video in this group:

Instructional/Informative

There are dozens you can make over time. Here are a few examples and suggestions:

- How to floss/use that fancy new electric toothbrush.
- Instructions for take home whitening.
- Make sure to use your insurance before year end.
- Updated safety protocols.
- Any instruction that is better as a visual.

As you can see, most of these will feature the team. These can be as simple as one person filming while one person talks/demonstrates.

These are good additions to your patient education library and they give people a chance to get to know the team. They are also good for SEO because these are frequently searched terms on Google and YouTube.

These will live on your YouTube channel (and possibly your site, depending on how comfortable you are adding video to your site). They should be captured horizontally for those platforms.

Just for Fun

I like to think of these as the David Attenborough videos—capturing you and the team in the Wild! This is you guys being you and doing the things a dental office team does.

- We went to continuing education.
- We celebrated a milestone—birthday/anniversary/new team/retirement.
- We're redecorating—or moving!
- We're doing a charity event.
- We're having a patient appreciation day.
- We're having a holiday party.

These are the least formal of all your videos and will be used almost exclusively in social media. It's good to know where you plan to use it before shooting. Some platforms favor vertical video—like Instagram stories, while Facebook prefers horizontal. (We'll cover those differences in **Part 2 - Using Your Videos**.)

Look at your weekly schedule and target people or events you want to capture so no one is scrambling at the last minute. Doing this will also enable you to capture some sort of one-off, fun video at least once a week. Video is rapidly outpacing pictures (and certainly just text) in social posting. Having a regular video presence will be increasingly important in getting noticed, liked, and engaged.

You don't need to create these all at once. They can be captured throughout the course of the year. If you do happen to get a couple on one day, don't post them all at once.

In **Part 2** we'll look at spreading out your awesomeness so it's always there.

So Many Videos - Even More Ways to Use Them

Videos are everywhere, and we know that people are more likely to engage with a video post than any other kind of content. They get shared, liked, and commented on more than pictures or text. As I said at the beginning, videos on social media generate 120 times more shares than images and texts.

In this section I will cover **YouTube** and its many backdoor tricks to getting your awesomeness found. I will provide step by step instruction with screenshots to make creating your channel, uploading, choosing the right title, and tagging your videos truly painless—and effective!

I'll also cover videos on social media; specifically Instagram and Facebook, as those two have the highest number of active users and are most commonly used by practices. If your practice is not on Instagram yet, I will quietly look away while you remedy that situation.

waiting...waiting

OK, did you open a business Insta account and link it to your business Facebook page? Well done!

If you're resisting Instagram because, "I already have Facebook and that's enough," let me share a few data points so you will see that although Facebook has been around forever, it's not the be-all and end-all of social media by a long shot.

A Selfstartr study (their spelling, not mine) showed that only 32% of Facebook users regularly interact with businesses, compared to 68% of Instagram users. Their final tally cites that businesses receive 58 times more engagement per follower on Instagram than Facebook.

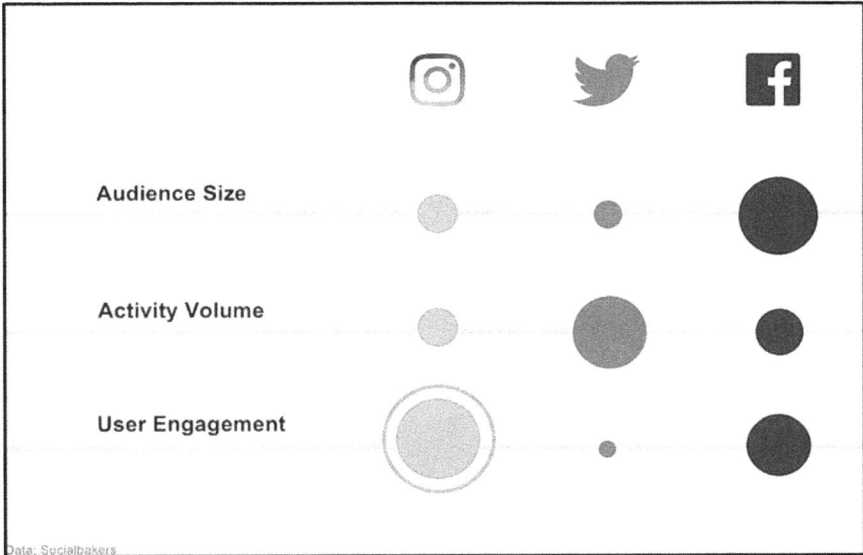

Data: Socialbakers

Facebook's algorithm also means that less than 6% of sponsored content gets seen by users. For Insta, it's almost 100%.

OK, I'm done lecturing you on Instagram. I know you've done the right thing.

Chapter 8 | Let's You This Tube!

I've told you that YouTube is the second most popular search engine in North America, so we've got to get your content on there, and then use some tricks to make sure you start showing up in searches.

First thing: Create a YouTube Channel

This is much easier than you think, and there's a surprisingly good chance you created one ages ago and forgot about it. I've seen that enough times to know it happens—A LOT. If you've ever worked with a marketing agency that handled content for you, they may have created one for you. Now you just need to find that login info they gave you…….

Either way, it pays to spend a few minutes doing a search on Google and YouTube to make sure you don't already have something there before you start from scratch.

Assuming you've found nothing, let's start at the beginning.

Step 1: Create a Google Account

Why? Because Alphabet, Google's parent company owns YouTube, and they get to make the rules about how to play in their sandbox. Not to worry—it's simple.

"For best results do all this set up on an actual computer. Some features, like customization, can't be done on mobile."
Pro Tip

Have you ever signed into Gmail, Google Maps, Google Play, or any other Google service? Great! You already have a Google account. In this case, you can skip ahead to Step 2.

Don't worry about the name and email address associated with your existing Google account being on-brand. Your existing Google account details won't be publicly linked with your YouTube account. The account is just the key to get you in the door—then we can redecorate the place.

If you don't have a Google account, here's how to create one.

This is the most up to date information as of printing. This being the internet, things will change, but the basic concept will remain.

Go to the **Google Account Creation** page. If typing in this address strikes you as crazy, you can also just Google it:

https://accounts.google.com/signup/v2/webcreateaccount?gmb=exp&biz=true&flowName=GlifWebSignIn&flowEntry=SignUp

You can choose to create a new Gmail address for your account or use your existing email address. Whichever you choose, *make sure it is owned by the practice owner*. You can give team members the ability to use it, but the owner MUST own the login credentials.

Just enter your details and click **Next**.

Step 2: Create a YouTube Brand Channel

With a personal YouTube account—which you get with that Google account—your channel has the same name as your Google account, meaning you can't use your brand name. Clearly, we want this to be all brand, all day.

When you create a **YouTube Brand Channel**, you can customize your channel with your branding, colors, logo, etc. A personal account limits who can manage your channel to only you. With a brand account you can give access to team members.

A brand channel also gives you access to YouTube analytics. This is a great tool to see who's watching your videos and what kind of content they respond to.

First, log into **YouTube** using your Google account details.

"Create your account on the desktop you plan to use for uploading and managing your content. It will then remember you next time. Otherwise, you will need to log in on each new device." **Pro Tip**

Then go to your YouTube channels page. You should see your personal account and a button that says **Create a Channel**—click that puppy!

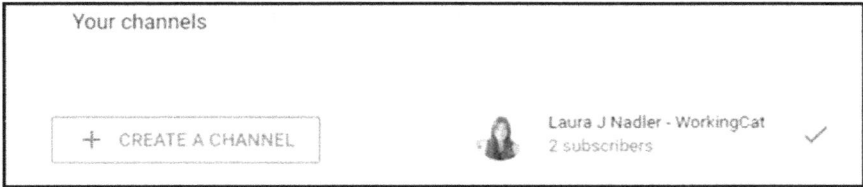

Enter your brand name (the name that will appear as your channel name) and click Create.

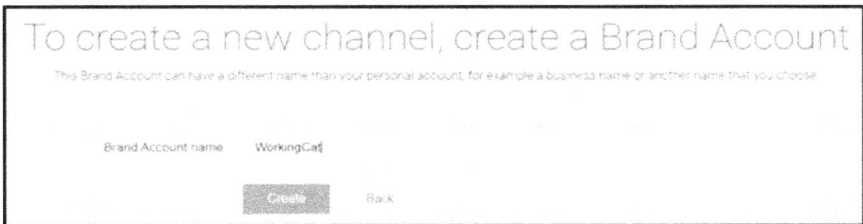

Nice work! You've got a YouTube Brand Channel for your practice. How easy was that?

Step 3: Make it All About You!

Click your **profile icon** on the top right of the screen and choose **Your channel**.

Click the blue **Customize Channel** button and select the **Branding** tab. That will take you here:

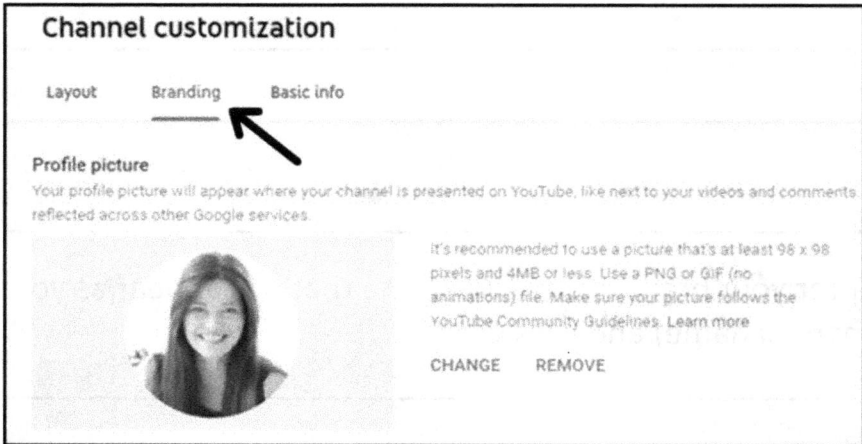

Channel customization

Layout   Branding   Basic info

Profile picture

Your profile picture will appear where your channel is presented on YouTube, like next to your videos and comments reflected across other Google services.

It's recommended to use a picture that's at least 98 x 98 pixels and 4MB or less. Use a PNG or GIF (no animations) file. Make sure your picture follows the YouTube Community Guidelines. Learn more

CHANGE   REMOVE

Upload your image and adjust the cropping as it guides you to. Use the same icon you use on your other social platforms. For most practices this will be your logo, but it might simply be a picture of the doc. Because I'm a professional speaker, my face is a big part of my brand, so my icons are my headshot, while my brand logo is in the banner image and on my watermark.

Next head down to the banner image.

Your brand logo is a good choice, although if your logo is compact rather than spread out horizontally like mine, the best fit is most likely the banner image from your website. This also provides a nice dose of brand consistency across platforms. You're probably using it as your Facebook or LinkedIn banner right now.

Note the size recommendations that YouTube provides.

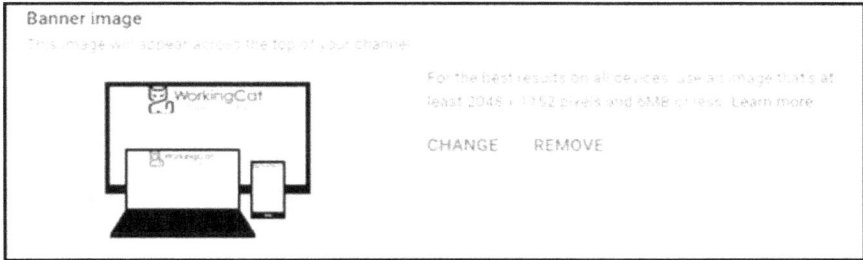

Add Links to Your YouTube Channel Banner

Click over to the **Basic Info** tab—the third one.

Here we're going to add info about your channel and links to your website and social media platforms. Think of the description box as the first step toward SEO. What might people be searching for that your channel would answer? Don't be all Keyword stuffy—use natural language. You have up to 1000 characters to tell your story.

We'll tackle actual keyword usage in **Chapter 10, "Advanced Stuff"** under **Channel Keywords.**

Provide that channel URL to your website provider so they can create a link to your channel on your site." **ProTip**

Add your website URL and any social platforms that you use to market your practice. YouTube will recognize the URL's and put the appropriate icons on your banner.

Chapter 9 | Show the World Your Awesomeness!

Let's Upload Those Videos

When someone arrives on your YouTube channel, your videos will show up in the reverse order in which you upload them—newest is first. This is why I recommend making your first upload the one you love the least. Over time it will be further down on the list. Some folks even make a quick to-camera video saying, "hey, we're here!" for just this purpose.

The good news is once you follow the steps below, you can ALWAYS go back and make changes to the things we're going to do or even "**Delete Forever**"—more on that later.

Soooo… head on over to the upper right of the screen where your profile image is and click that **CREATE** button.

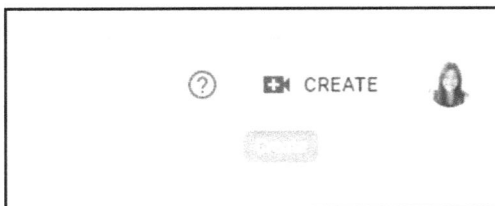

You'll see two options: **Go Live** (yikes!) and **Upload Videos**—let's upload. This will open a pop-up window. Click **Select Files** and then go choose your video from your files. Once the video uploads, a window with *so many blank fields* will appear. Don't panic—we're going to cover the ones you actually need to worry about. I'll show you the box empty now, and all filled in later.

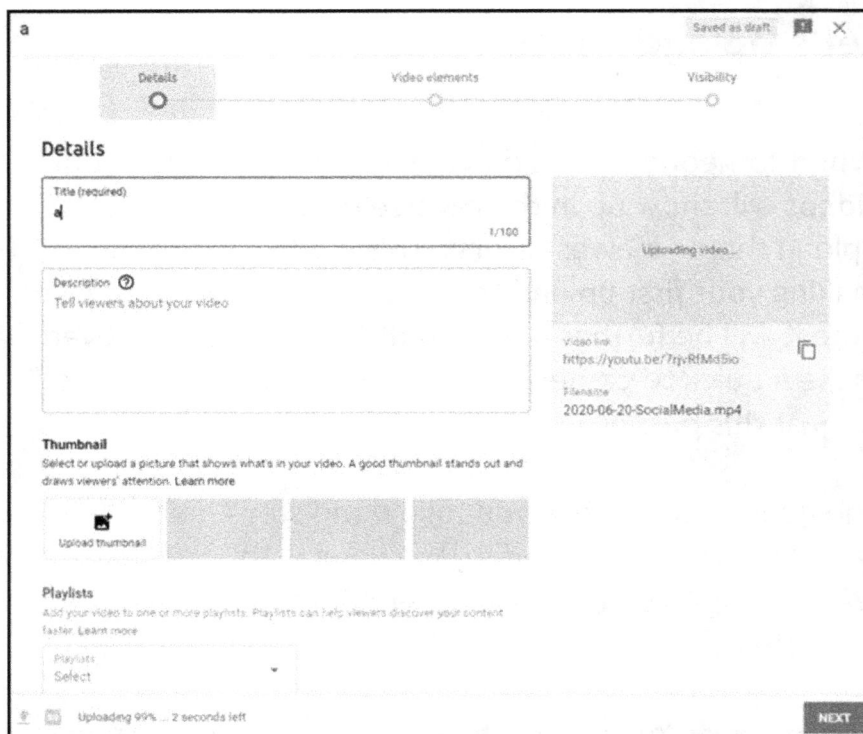

Title: Always start this with your practice name. This is for consistency and brand recognition. I like to use the vertical line to separate the brand from the title, but you can use whatever you like (colon, dash, etc.) Just pick one and stick with it. For example:

Paradise Dental | In-Office Whitening

Description: Keep it short and sweet. Too many people want to tell the whole story of the video here. So, let's take a quick survey:

I go to YouTube to:

A. Watch Videos   B. Read (really?)

Thought so. Nobody is reading more than what shows up in those 2-3 visible lines under a video, because they have to click "See More", and again, nobody's here to read.

That means we need to maximize those first couple of lines with the info we want people to see all the time: Practice name, website URL and a call to action with your phone number. "Call us to learn about whitening." "Book your appointment today!" Make sure the call to action is appropriate to the video—no whitening comments on an Invisalign video. You get the idea.

"When adding your website, don't just type it in. You want it to create a hyperlink that will be clickable under your video. Do this by opening your site and copying the URL, then pasting it in." **Pro Tip**

Thumbnail: This is the still image that will appear in search. You will have three to choose from. Yes, I know, they all feature closed eyes and open mouths. We'll cover **Custom Thumbnails** in the **"Advanced Stuff"** Chapter under **Verify Your Account.** For now, pick the one you can live with. You can always come back and change it.

Audience: On this part of the page, you'll have to tick a box stating whether your video is made for kids or not. It's not a trick question, nor is it an MPAA rating thing—it's not about there being adult content. It's actually just the opposite—it's about kid specific content. Unless you are making a kid specific video, you want to tick NO.

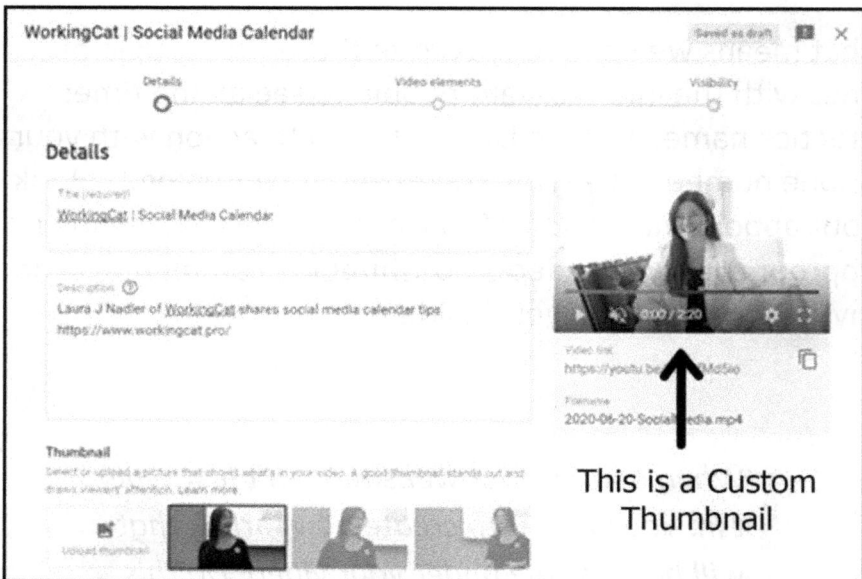

This is a Custom Thumbnail

Scroll down to find **Show More** and click that to reveal **Tags**—about 2/3 of the way down.

This is where we'll add those behind-the-scenes words that get your video found.

Tags are like keywords for your video. Even though it seems like Google knows everything about you and every move you make, they don't currently scrape video for content that tells them what your video is about. You have to do this. Unlike the description, you can add a whole lot here, but don't go overboard. You will max out around 400 characters. Viewers do not see these tags.

Tags for Every Video

- Who are You? Doc and/or practice name
- What do you do? Dentist/dentistry
- Where are you? Your city/town and/or significant landmarks
- What's this video about? In my example on page 59, it's about using a social media calendar

A note on the landmark thing. I mean *well-known landmarks,* like tourist attractions that are within view, or things that people reference in directions. "Make a left at the Marina." "We're across from Central Park". If you use it when you talk about your practice, use it here, otherwise stick with your city/town. For example, Millennium Park Dental in Chicago definitely uses Millennium Park and "The Bean", but a practice somewhere down Michigan Avenue should not.

In the *what's it about* category, you want to think about what people type to search, and tailor your tags to that. That means simple tags like "social media calendar" **and** long-tail keywords like "how to use a social media calendar".

Long-tail keywords became very important in Google's last algorithm update, because so many people now use voice search which involves more "natural language".

"Keep in mind how patients talk about dental procedures. We call it Whitening, but many patients call it Bleaching—make sure to use both in your tags. Same with crowns and caps." **Pro Tip**

In our Wonderful World of Dental we sometimes have blinders on about our terminology. If you're talking about implants, make sure to use "dental implants".

Plain "implants" brings up a whole other kind of search result. 😳

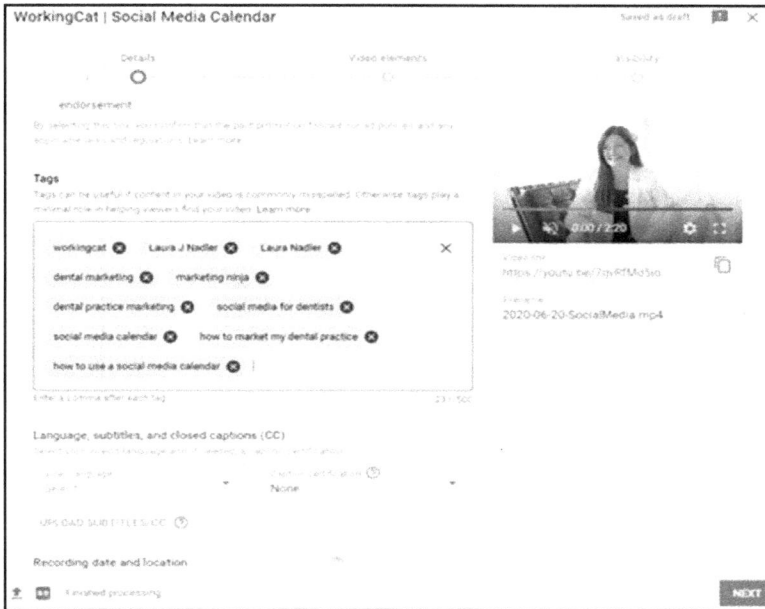

Finally, make it **Public** then don't forget to hit that all important **Publish** button!

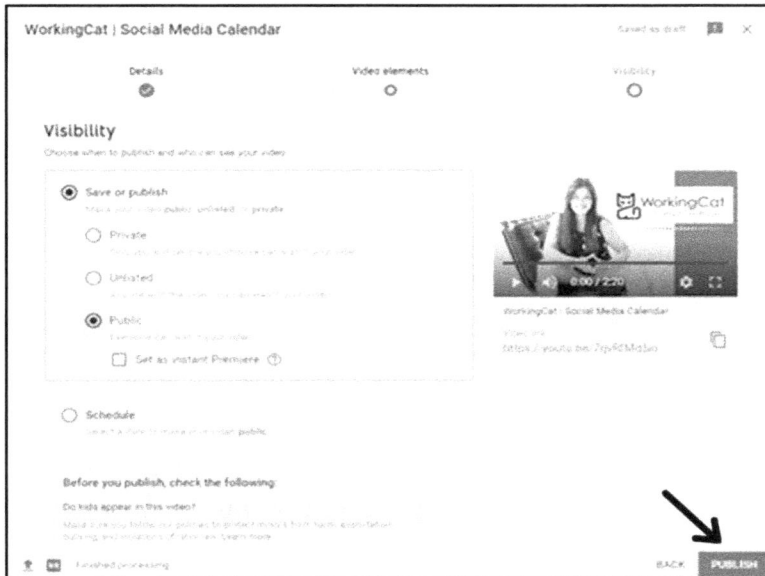

You'll be given a pop-up option to share to other platforms, and if sharing this video now is in line with your social media calendar, then by all means, share away! If not, just close that pop-up.

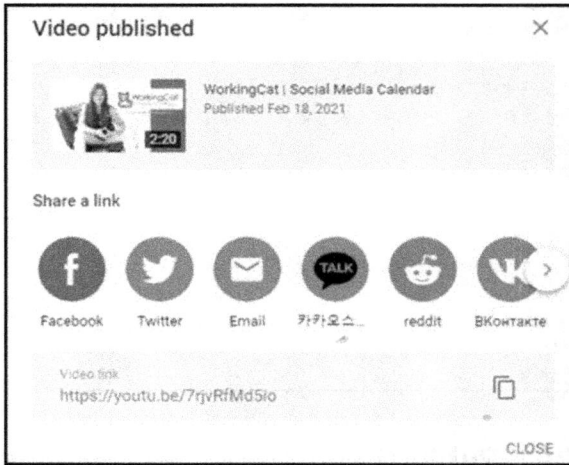

Now this video will show up on your channel like this:

If you hover over this listing, it will bring up a few symbols. The first one you want to click is the red **YouTube symbol** ▶. This lets you view your video on the platform the way a viewer or subscriber would see it.

Specifically, you are looking below the video and title to the "about" section to make sure that your website URL has rendered as a hyperlink and that clicking on it takes you to your site.

You can also click on the **Pencil** to make edits to all the things we just did—or add more tags as you think of them.

Clicking on the **3 stacked dots** for more options is where you will find a shareable link for this video so you can share it to other platforms later, and that somehow sad sounding **Delete Forever** I mentioned earlier.

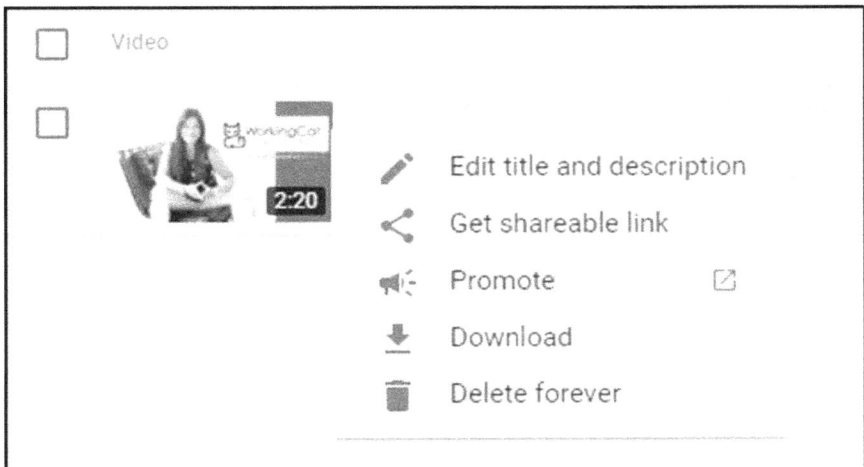

Wow – You Did It!

Good job! That first one's a doozy, but now it's there for all the world to see.

If you've never done anything like this before it may have seemed like a lot of steps, but I promise, the more you do the easier it will be. Plus, you only have to create and personalize the channel once.

If you're up for it now, this is a good time to look at some advanced steps that will let you enable features like adding other team members, so they can handle uploads and such in the future.

Chapter 10 | Advanced Steps

Add Team Members

For most of my clients I recommend adding one or two people as Managers. If Luis is on vacation, then Yvonne can take over. If your team is small, or if the doctor/owner plans to be an active participant in uploads and such, then you can just have one.

Sign into your YouTube channel
From the menu on the left, choose **Settings** at the bottom.
Click on **Permissions**.
Click **Manage permissions** in the top section.

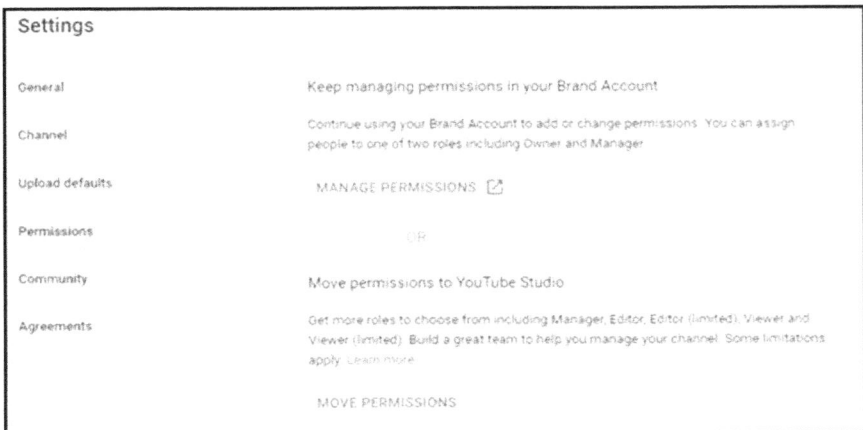

Settings	
General	Keep managing permissions in your Brand Account
Channel	Continue using your Brand Account to add or change permissions. You can assign people to one of two roles including Owner and Manager.
Upload defaults	MANAGE PERMISSIONS [↗]
Permissions	OR
Community	Move permissions to YouTube Studio
Agreements	Get more roles to choose from including Manager, Editor, Editor (limited), Viewer and Viewer (limited). Build a great team to help you manage your channel. Some limitations apply. Learn more.
	MOVE PERMISSIONS

That will bring you to **Brand Account details**. Click **Manage Permissions**.

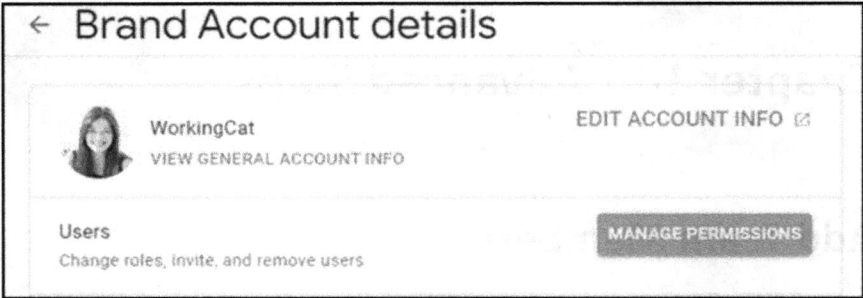

Click that tiny little **people icon** in the top right to invite new users.

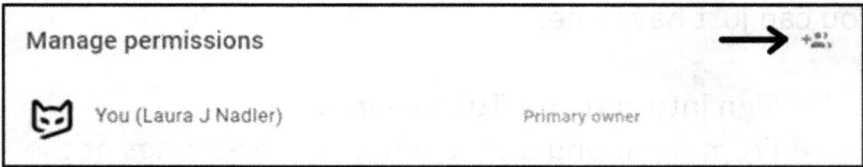

Enter the email addresses of the team members you want to add to your account. For each person, you need to choose a role.

Owners can take any action on the account, including deleting the account and adding new users.

Managers can post videos. **Managers** is how you want to add team members Click **Invite**, then **Done**. They will be able to log in to the channel now.

Channel Trailer

A channel trailer is a short video introducing your practice to new visitors to your channel. Use it to show them what you're all about and why they should watch your videos and subscribe to your channel. This can be a shortened, edited-together version of your Meet the Doc and Meet the Team, or your Hero video with a voice over explaining your practice or your mission statement. See all the places that one comes in handy?

Here's how to add a YouTube channel trailer of your own.

Log into YouTube and upload the video you want to use. Then go to your channel and click **Customize Channel**. Go to the first tab, **Layout.**

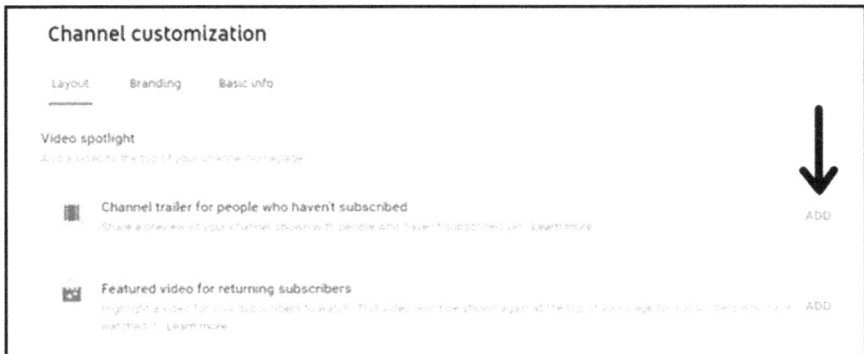

Click **ADD**, then select your video from the window that pops up.

If you're really popular on YouTube with tons of returning subscribers, you can add a **Featured Video** as well. For most people, this isn't necessary.

Channel Keywords

Although we've added tags to your videos, we want to make sure people can find your channel too. This will put all your awesomeness on display at once. This can also add another listing of you in search, because while your website and socials should all show up, we want your channel and your videos to show up as well. The more listings you have on a search page, the more likely people are to click, because it reads as "authority" in the space.

How to Add Channel Keywords

- Sign into your YouTube channel
- From the menu on the left, choose **Settings** at the bottom.
- Click on **Channel**. Then chose the **Basic Info** tab.
- In the **Keywords** section, enter terms relevant to your content. Be sure to focus only on keywords that truly relate to the content you plan to produce. Don't say "holistic dentist" if you're not. Think about what your ideal patient is searching for, and make sure your keywords—and content—match that.

- If you misspell something, click on the X in the oval next to the keyword to delete it. Use normal word spacing—do not string words together like a hashtag:

dentalpracticemarketing is not a keyword.

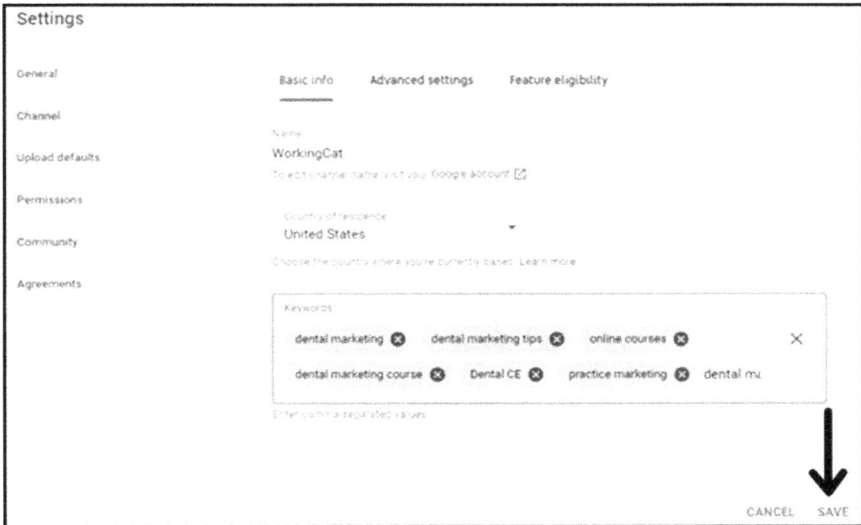

Always remember to hit **Save**. Like all the other places, you can always come back here to add or delete as needed.

Verify Your Account

You need to verify your YouTube account to be able to upload videos longer than 15 minutes (not that you should have videos this long—but who knows) and to create custom thumbnails for your videos. Have your mobile phone at hand for this.

Go to **youtube.com/verify**

Choose your country.

Chose the Text option—it's just quicker

Enter your mobile number.

Enter the verification code you receive via text and click **Submit**.

WooHoooo! You're verified.

Now the options to upload longer videos and create custom thumbnails are enabled on your channel.

That's a wrap on the specifics of YouTube. In the rest of the book I'm going to cover the social media platforms and their specific types of videos.

This might be a good time to digest what we've covered before we jump into all things social.

Chapter 11 | Let's Get Social!

Alrighty then, that's enough YouTube for one book! Let's talk about the platforms that you probably already use IRL (in real life)—Facebook and Instagram. In this section I'll describe the types of videos on each platform and how and when to best use them. There is also a chapter devoted to formatting and specs for each platform, because the tech nerd in me knows some of you will want to know that stuff.

A quick word about **TikTok**. Yes, this platform is the land of video, but I am not covering it in this book for a variety of reasons. The #1 reason is that I want you to ACTUALLY USE video, and adding another new thing to learn will lead to overwhelm. In my years of coaching clients, I have learned that if we add too many things to the mix, very few get done. Let's focus on the core platforms and make our content on them amazing!

You can always add TikTok—or whatever fabulous new platform is being developed as I write this—in the future. My one exception would be a pedo or ortho office who sees mostly 10–16-year-olds. YOU should be on TikTok— it's where the cool kids are.

For everyone else: master one thing at a time, add as you feel comfortable. Do not feel the need to jump on every new platform. Many don't last, and devoting time to them will burn you out.

"Designate a phone or tablet in the practice to be used for posting. That way anyone can grab the moment, even if one person is handling the posting later. It doesn't need to be a working cell phone. Hook that old phone up to Wifi and it'll work just as well as any others, with no monthly fees." **Pro Tip**

The next two chapters will walk you through the various options for video on Facebook and Instagram as of this publication.

Again, start at the beginning and get familiar with one or two types of content sharing. You don't need to use all of these every day—honestly, you'd scare followers away if you did.

Play around and see which work best for your practice. Your content will see greater engagement if you do one or two things well and consistently than if you do them all not so well.

Chapter 12 | The Elephant

FaceBook

There are two primary uses for video here: **In-Feed** and **Lives**. Fortunately, they were given pretty self-evident names. 😉 For the purpose of practice marketing, you will use In-Feed most of the time.

In-Feed Videos

This is where you can post virtually any kind of video content from short clips to full length features. As with your YouTube video, I recommend sticking to 2 minutes or less. You can certainly show off your fabulous Evergreens here—and I recommend that you do—but as you've surely seen on Facebook, most people are grabbing a phone, capturing a video, and sharing.

I recommend showcasing all your Evergreen videos over the course of several weeks and then mix in the less produced ones. You don't want to put up all the high-end quality first and then only have the quickies to share. You'll lose engagement.

A great idea is featuring them during a celebration day or week. Show your *Meet the Admin Team* in April for Admin Professional's Day, or your *Meet the Doc* on March 6th for Dentist's Day, and so on.

Consider your audience when deciding how to hold your phone for these quick videos.

Are most of your patients "mature"? Then go with that horizontal image since they are more often going to be viewing it on a desktop.

Is your patient base more millennial? They're checking in on a phone—100%—so go vertical.

If you're split, stick with the horizontal here on Facebook since the younger crowd is more likely to find and follow you on Instagram, anyway. Most of my clients fall in the mature category, so I stick with that 16:9 horizontal for my Facebook video posts.

Brilliant weekend with the folks of the American College of...
a year ago · 16 Views

Laura J Nadler CE Seminar
2 years ago · 46 Views

SEO v. SEM
3 years ago · 16 Views

I tell my clients that they should be posting to their social platforms at least 3 times a week—I'd prefer 4-5. If you're maintaining that 3ish level, make at least one of those a video. Posting every day? Go you!! Make at least 2 of those videos.

These can be as quick and simple as "Hey! Here's Cleopatra, our VIP patient of the week with the beautiful bouquet we gave here!" Always remember to add your call to action (CTA). "Call us for an appointment. Maybe you will be our *next* VIP!"

Any time the team does something besides practicing dentistry is an opportunity to snap a quick video. People LOVE seeing you in your natural habitat. It makes you human and easier to relate to. Be sure to include parties, team birthdays, CE events, dental shows, and any charity work you do. That last one gets tremendous engagement. Remember to tag these as you would any picture. #dentallife

Facebook Lives

There is a lot to be said for the Facebook Live in many areas of business and marketing. That said, since you are practicing during the day when patients are likely working, it can be a major challenge to execute a Live at time that works for you and for your intended audience.

The most effective place to do a Live is in lieu of a live informational meeting. For example, I know a practice that, pre-COVID, regularly did informational seminars in their office on things like implants, Invisalign, etc. During the pandemic they wanted to continue to provide the content—it was very effective at converting patients—so they turned to FB Lives. Since they normally held these seminars in the evening, shifting to virtual made sense, and patients were used to interacting with them at those times.

So if the Live Bug bites you, go for it! The great thing about a Live is that a recording of it will live on your Facebook page so you can remind people it's available even if they missed you... Live.

Plan to go no more than 10-15 minutes on your first Live. Have notes in front of you—there's no editing when you're live. When you're ready to start, go to your page and click on **Live**.

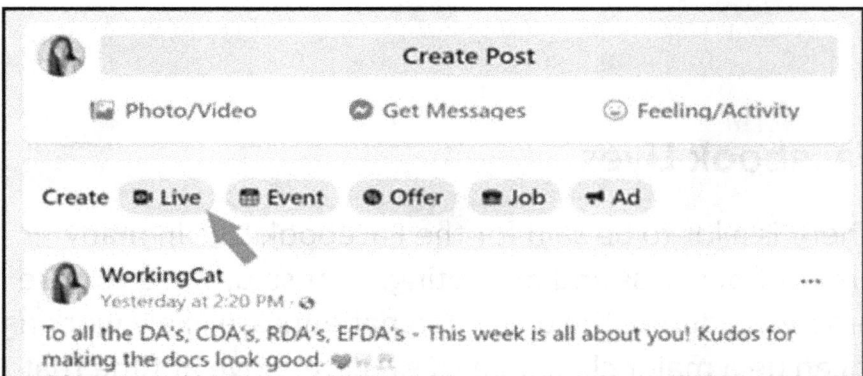

Live Producer

- Go Live Now
- Go Live With Others
- Schedule a Live Video
- Upcoming Live Videos & Events

Post

WorkingCat

Post to Page you manage ▾

WorkingCat ▾

Title (Required)

Say something about this live

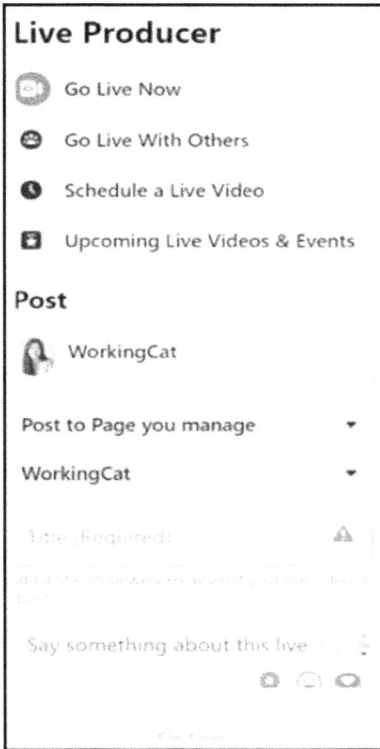

You will be able to see how you look, and make any adjustments to your lighting, background (remember The Stuff) and how you're framed.

Be sure to add a title and a quick note about what you plan to cover.

Once you hit Start, a 3 second count down will start on the screen. Once it's done counting, you're LIVE!

If people hop on your Live, remember to acknowledge them as you speak— "Hi, Laura!" If things get REALLY busy have a team member reply for you in the comments.

It's a good idea to answer questions live as people type them in the comments. This will keep them engaged and more likely to attend any future Lives you do.

Once you're done, FB will automatically keep a recording and prompt you to add comments, etc. to the post. This will now appear in your feed and in your stored videos on the left of your page.

That's it! Again, it's not hard to do, just consider your audience and your message when deciding if a Live is the best option.

Chapter 13 | The Gram

Instagram

When Instagram first started back in October of 2010 it was the place to share all your photos. It was so successful that less than 2 years later Facebook bought the emerging platform rather than try to compete or copy it. Despite that ownership, Insta has managed to keep its best features to itself, and many of those now take the form of video rather than just pics. Let's talk about each of those and how they fit into your marketing mix.

Instagram In-Feed and Carousel Videos

In Feed

These are the things that show up in the main part of your feed, or as it's often called on your profile, The Grid. These are the square images you see as you scroll through your feed or go to a profile page. You can either upload videos from your phone, or record directly in the app.

Like regular photo posts these will stay there on your grid unless you delete them. Follow the same guidelines as the chapter on Facebook for what to post and how often.

To upload a video or record a new one:

Tap the plus icon as you would for a regular post.

- To upload a video from your phone's library, click on the down arrow next to **Gallery** to reveal your options. Chose **Videos**. Select the video you'd like to share.
- To record a new video in the app, tap the camera image above your phone's gallery/ library. Tap and hold the center circle to start recording—lift your finger to stop.

Keep in mind that the maximum video length is 60 seconds. Once you've recorded or uploaded a video, you can apply a filter, add a caption and location just like you would with a photo.

"Although you can use a desktop app for posting photos to Insta, you can't take or upload videos from a desktop computer."
Pro Tip

Carousel

This is where you see multiple images in the same post in a feed. You can upload up to 10 photos and videos and share them as a single post. Notice I said upload. These are going to be videos that already exist on your phone. Multiple videos recorded in app will be covered in Stories.

To upload multiple images or videos:

- To start, tap that little plus at the top to view your phone's library.
- Tap that little icon that looks like a stack of papers (it's next to the camera icon).
- Select up to 10 photos and videos from your phone's library. To adjust how each photo or video is cropped, tap it then touch the screen to adjust how it fits in the frame. Then tap Next in the lower right.
- Tap a filter at the bottom of the screen to apply it to every photo and video you've selected or tap a photo or video to edit it and add filters individually.
- To change the order of your photos and videos, tap and hold one then drag it to another spot. To remove a photo or video from your post, tap and hold one, then drag it to the trashcan. When you're done, tap Next in the top right.
- Tap Share.

"The orientation you choose (square, portrait or landscape) affects all of the photos or videos in your post. You can't select a different orientation for each photo or video." **Pro Tip**

Keep in mind that posts containing multiple videos may take longer to upload, so make sure you're connected to a reliable network—and maybe not burn through your data!

Instagram Stories, Hi-lights and IGTV

When Instagram added Stories in 2016 the platform got so much more fun! It let users start recording one-off videos or collections of images that disappear in 24 hours—unless you save them to Hi-Lights!
Stories allow you to add so many customizations and creative elements to tell your story. Another big advantage to Stories is that they appear at the top of the feed—no need to scroll to see them. Once someone clicks on one of those story circles, the app auto-plays through all of them so you're more likely to get seen.
If this is your first Story, remember this: no one sees until you hit share. Play around, try all the crazy options. If you don't like it, trash it. No one will ever know. Except me—I know things.

To create your story:

- Swipe right anywhere from your feed, then scroll to Story at the bottom. Usually that's where it lands as soon as you swipe.
- Tap and hold that center circle at the bottom of the screen to record your video.
- To choose a video from your phone's library or gallery instead, swipe up anywhere on the screen and pick the one you want to use.
- Those fun little symbols at the top let you draw, add text, a sticker—even gifs—to your video. To remove one you decide against, drag and drop it into the trashcan at the bottom of the screen.
- You can also use them to tag folks, add a survey, ask a question, etc.
- When you're ready to share, tap **Your Story** in the bottom left.

*"To take a video with a camera effect— AKA **Filters**, swipe left at the bottom of the screen and select an effect. You can also swipe all the way to the left and tap the search to see more effects from Instagram and from independent creators". **Pro Tip***

Assuming you've linked your Business Facebook page, it will share to both, though I have yet to meet someone who says, "OMG—did you see that amazing Facebook Story?", so don't sweat that.

Did you notice all those symbols on the left when you swiped to Story? So many fun options there. My personal favorite is **Hands-Free**. This is particularly helpful if you're planning to record for a little bit, or if you're like me and you talk with your hands. Who wants to hold that circle down the whole time you're recording?

Some of those options are:

- **Boomerang** to take a burst of photos that loops forward and backward.
- **Superzoom** to take a video that automatically zooms in on an object and plays a dramatic sound. Tap anywhere on the screen to select an area or object to zoom in on, then tap the circle at the bottom to start recording.
- **Create** to personalize a story without needing a photo or video to start from. You can type something, add a GIF, or ask a question, take a survey or many other things.

Should it be a Feed Post or a Story?

There are a few things to consider when deciding which format to use. For example, most users scroll through their Feed with the sound off (I know I do!) while around 70% of Stories are watched with the sound on. Is sound integral to you what you want to post?
Let's consider some of the real—and perceived—differences between Feed and Story:

The Feed is best for content that is:

- **Evergreen** - Content that you want patients to be able to see "forever".
- **Curated** - Valuable content with good quality images. Very on-brand.
- **Far Reaching** - Posts are more likely to reach new audiences than Stories because they get more heavily hash-tagged.

In general, your feed posts should include content about your technology, team, office, or philosophy, and should have an overall look and vibe that matches your brand.

Stories tend to be:

- **Timely** - Since they only last 24 hours, they can be more "in the moment".
- **Casual** - Selfie or "behind-the-scenes" videos are hugely popular.

- **Designed for engagement** - Your Stories will be watched by your current followers.

This is a good place for those "Look at us at a CE course!" videos, short-term promos or even polls and surveys. I know where I live, it's super useful for letting patients know when you'll be closed for snow days. Or lizards...

Instagram Lives

Much of the same criteria for Facebook Lives applies here, with the exception that people are more likely to get an alert on their phone that you've started a **Live** (if they follow you) so you have a better chance of people watching it. The user demographics of Instagram also skew more toward people who are willing to watch a **Live** when it pops up, so if your patient demographic is a bit younger this is the place to try out a Live.

*"Younger isn't what it used to be. A lot of Millennials are 40+ now, and they are Insta's heart and soul. Don't think you need patients under 30 for this!"—**Pro Tip***

To start a Live broadcast from the Instagram app

- Tap the plus sign at the top or swipe right anywhere in Feed like you did for Stories, then scroll to **Live** at the bottom.
- To add a title, tap **Title** on the left and enter a title, then tap **Add Title**.
- Tap the icon at the bottom that looks like sound emitting from a dot. The number of viewers appears at the top of the screen and comments appear at the bottom.
- You will get a 3 second count-down, so wait for it before you start talking.
- You can add a comment by tapping **Comment** at the bottom of the screen.
- Tap a comment and tap **Pin Comment** to pin it so that viewers can see it more easily.
- When you're done, tap **End** in the top right then tap to confirm. From there, you can tap the down arrow in the top left to save it to your camera roll or share it to **IGTV**.

Keep in mind that when you save your live broadcast to your IGTV or download the broadcast from Live Archive, only the broadcast is saved, and not things like comments, likes and viewers. It may take a minute for your live broadcast to save to your phone, especially for longer videos.

Reels

Reels are the newest addition to the IG video family, and aren't they cute? Reels were created as the Facebook and Instagram answer to **TikTok**—short, produced videos with a fun edge. If you happen to be a TikTok user, you will see a lot of those videos repurposed in Reels.

Reels allows you to record and edit short videos up to 30 seconds in the Instagram Camera. You can add effects and music to your reel or use your own original audio.

To make these directions clearer, this is the Reels Icon:

And these are the arrows that are used in Reels:

To record a Reel from the Instagram app:

- Tap the **Reels** icon at the bottom, then tap the camera icon at the top. Alternately, you can also tap the plus at the top, then scroll to **Reels** at the bottom.
- Tap and hold the **Reels** icon to record a clip or tap it to start recording and tap it again to end the clip. You can also tap your camera roll in the bottom left to add a video from your camera roll.
- Tap the back arrow to watch, trim or delete the previous clip you recorded.

- Tap the forward arrow to add stickers, drawings and text to your reel or download it to your device. Use the slider at the bottom to edit when you want text to appear.
- Tap the forward arrow, then tap **Cover** to change your cover photo and write a caption. Tap **Stories** at the top if you want to share your reel to your story instead of to **Explore**.
- Tap **Share**, then tap **Done**.

Note that you can record one or multiple clips that add up to 30 seconds. The progress bar at the top shows how long you've recorded. If you share your reel to **Explore**, it can also be seen on the **Reels** section of your profile. **Explore** will make your Reels discoverable to the wide world. It will also display it in your **Grid**.

Keep in mind, you won't be able to use **interactive** stickers (example: poll, Q&A, challenge) in your Reel.

Other fun Reel options:

When you record a Reel, you'll see a tool menu on the left. You can tap:

- **The Music Note** to search for a song in your music library. You can choose which part of the song you want to play.
- **The Fast Forward** to change the speed of your reel. This will affect both the video and audio of your clip.
- **The Smile with Sparkles** to add a camera effect. Swipe left at the bottom of the screen and select an effect. To see more effects, swipe all the way to the left and tap the magnifying glass with sparkles. Yes, Instagram has a thing for sparkles.
- **The Stopwatch** to choose the length of your clip. When you return to your clip, you will see a countdown before your clip starts recording. This is useful if you know you want to go shorter than the 30 second limit.
- **The Multiple Image Icon** to see the end of your last clip. You can use the transparent photo to align your next clip before recording the next bit. This will only appear after you record your first clip. How cool is THAT feature??

Note that you can also record a Reel with your own audio, so you're not limited to the music library.

Reels may seem like a lot of work, but once you get the hang of it, they're pretty easy. Instagram is constantly evolving, so staying up on the new features will definitely serve you and your practice marketing. In the first year they existed, only a few people used Stories. Now people post to Stories more than the Feed. I would expect Reels to see that same uptick—especially for businesses—as users' desire for produced and curated content increases.

I know Instagram gives you a lot of options. My best advice is to try them one at a time. You may find you like the quick, "right now" aspect of Stories, or you may be a fabulous creative who thrives on the production aspect of Reels.

Don't feel you need to use all of them all the time, but do at least try them. It's like the Lottery – you never know!

Chapter 14 | Nitty Gritty Techy Things

File Sizes and Formats for Each Social

This chapter is here because I know some of you will want to know all the details before you so much as touch these platforms. For the rest of you, this might seem like...pulling teeth—oh no, she didn't!

Millions of people use these platforms without ever thinking about file size or aspect ratio, but if there's one thing I've learned about dentists it's that they like all the details.

You are NOT, however, allowed to get bogged down in this and have it derail your plans for online video stardom. I have spoken.

The file sizes in each group refer to videos you upload. If you are recording within a given platform (Lives, Stories), you don't need to think about those numbers—yeah!—because the platform optimizes it for you.

Facebook Feed Video

Recommended size: 1280 by 720 pixels
Minimum width: 600 pixels

Supported aspect ratios:

- 16:9 (horizontal): This is the most common aspect for FB on desktop, and conveniently, it's how you shot your Evergreens. This is also how **FB Lives** will appear.
- 9:16 (full portrait): You've seen these—they have those fuzzy backgrounds on both sides on a desktop, but they translate well to mobile, so consider your audience. If you share from Insta, this is how it will look.
- 2:3 (vertical), 4:5 (vertical), square (1:1): Not used as much but handy if you want to reuse 1:1 footage from Insta.

Recommended specs: .MP4 or .MOV format, but it will support most types of video files. Your videos can be as long as 240 minutes (but remember, we're not creating feature films here so stick to that 2 minute or less mark), and as large as 4GB.

Instagram In-Feed and Carousel Videos

Recommended size: 1080 by 1080 pixels
Minimum size: 600 by 600 pixels

Supported aspect ratios:

1:1: You know, **The Grid**. Square videos take up 78% more real estate in a person's mobile feed than a 16:9 video. You want them to SEE you, so take up all the real estate you can!
4:5: Known as **Portrait**, can also appear in your feed— there will be empty space on the sides.

Recommended specs: .MP4 or .MOV format, maximum length 60 seconds, but you can string multiple 60 second clips together in a Carousel.

The **Carousel** allows viewer to swipe through multiple pictures and/or video clips in one frame of the feed. You can now include up to 10.

According to Instagram, square video (1:1) results in 30-35% more video views and an 80-100% (!) more engagement than landscape video (16:9).

Instagram Stories, Hi-lights and IGTV

Recommended size: 1080 by 1920 pixels
Minimum size: 600 by 1067 pixels

Supported aspect ratios:

- 9:16: The one everyone uses because it takes up the full vertical screen.

- 4:5: Second best, and you can add things outside the frame in the blank space.
- 16:9: I would never use this because most people use Insta on mobile and this will make your video a tiny strip across their screen.

Recommended specs: .MP4 or .MOV format.

The maximum length for individual **Story** clip is 15 seconds (but you can string a boatload together to tell a bigger story), maximum file size 4GB. When you're recording, just keep going. It will break it up into those little clips for you.

"As you get more comfortable shooting Stories, you will learn to pause at that 15 second mark so the transition is super smooth." **Pro Tip**

IGTV can be as short as 15 seconds or as long as an hour. The maximum file size for videos 10 minutes or less is 650MB and 3.6GB for 60-minute videos.

You can also save your **Lives** to **IGTV** as soon as you finish recording. You will be given the option right away. This shows a series of my lives saved to IGTV.

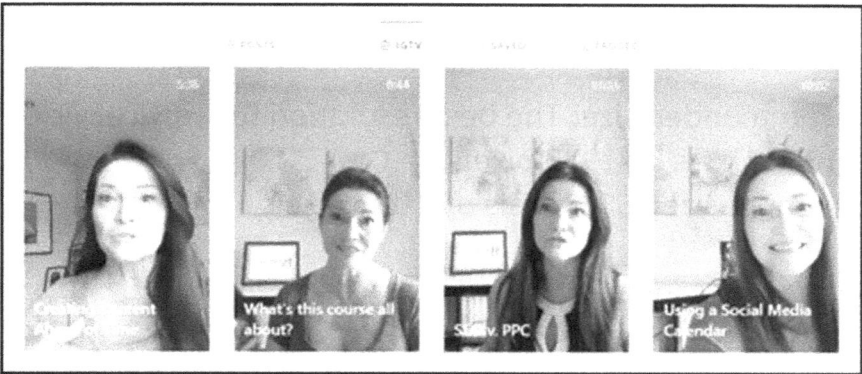

Instagram Lives:

The platform will dictate the sizes as your record.
These are all 9:16.
They can be a maximum of 60 minutes.

Lives in Your Grid

In your Feed and on your Grid your Lives will show up in the standard 1:1, so keep that in mind when you're shooting. Try to keep the focus of your image in the middle. This shows you how that first IGTV (from above) looks in my grid:

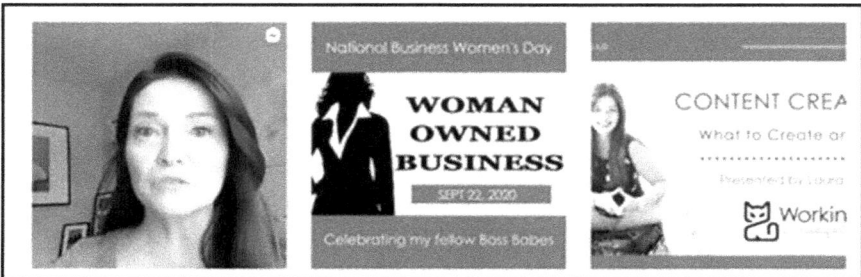

Reels

Recommended size: The best resolution for vertical videos is 1080 pixels by 1920 pixels.
Minimum size: 600 pixels by 1067 pixels.

Supported aspect ratios:

- 9:16: That full vertical screen but remember that it will show up in the feed and on the Grid as a square—just like the Lives.

The file format should be. MP4 or. MOV, 30 seconds, maximum file size is 4GB.

Chapter 15 | You Got This!

I know we covered a lot in those 14 chapters. I hope it got you to try new things. I hope you became familiar and even comfortable with the ins and outs of the platforms. Some may become your go-to outlets. Others may have made you say, "Nope, not for me."

Mostly, I hope you create and share videos you are proud of that truly showcase what makes your practice special.

That's the real reason to do this. To create and use assets that tell your story so you attract the patients who will most appreciate your practice. Not every practice is for every patient, and I know you've had patients who you decided were not for you.

By telling the story of who you are in practice, you give prospective patients a window into your beliefs and strengths. This helps them make informed decisions about who provides their care.

If you got to have a bit of fun along the way—even better.

I know that even after all these step-by-step instructions and a bazillion screen shots there may be questions. At WorkingCat Marketing this is what we do. If you want to talk with us don't be shy.

And if you bump into me at a dental show, say hi!

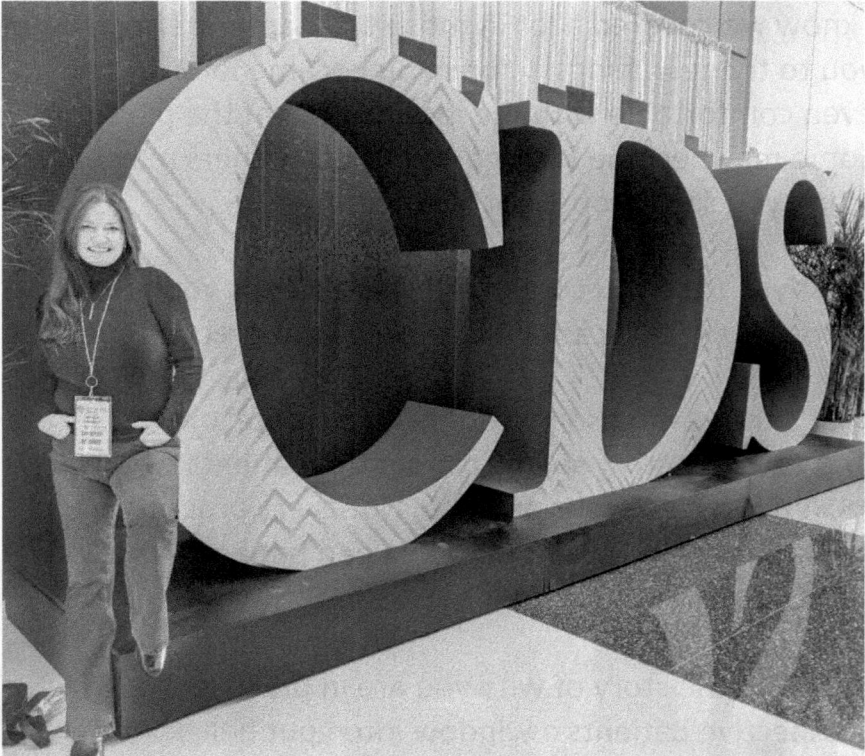

...and make sure you post it!

Acknowledgements

So many people have come into my life whose words, influence and friendship led to me writing this book. I'm sure I've missed some, but here are the ones on my mind today:

- Lynette Schwanger, the Producer for all my clients' professional videos. She is a PRO!
- Dear clients for whom we produced videos, including, but not limited to Bryan Griffith and his epic team, Steve Hudis and Jeannie, Laura Dyras and Laura and Shanna.
- Joseph R. Morris DDS, a dear friend who also happens to be an amazing dentist (and actor!)
- Tina Tower and her Empire Builders Mastermind – especially that first little group who banded together despite COVID and still cheer each other on: Helen, Karen, Michelle, Farien.
- My tribe at SCN, especially Judy Kay Mausolf, Janice Hurley and Rita Zamora for always being engaged.
- Teams who've attended my courses over the years and asked so many good questions. They always make me go back to see what I can add and what better value I can bring to my clients.
- Liz Armato – for a billion things – but especially for her friendship.

And lastly – but mostly – my husband Jason. He has supported my dreams, goals, delusions and plans for world domination for almost 3 decades. He told me I should write a book years ago. He's often right. Don't tell him I said that. He also writes amazing fiction. You can find him at JHNadler.com

About the Author

I'm an international speaker and the founder of WorkingCat Marketing, which focuses on practice marketing for dentists and elective healthcare. I've worked with hundreds of clients around the globe, and also present an online practice marketing course called "From Found to Five Stars".

Over the years I've been delighted to share my expertise with organizations like Pride Institute, Sesame Communications, Spear Study Clubs, American College of Prosthodontists, SCN, ASCA, Denmat, DentechChina, Tufts University School of Dental Medicine, Boston University, University at Sea, and many others.

When I'm not saving the dental world from bad marketing, you'll find me traveling for fun—14 countries, 3 continents and counting! I am a card-carrying sci-fi and word nerd and a lover of good food and wine. I've written for both the food and wine industry and the film industry—and appeared in the commercial for Words with Friends. Seeing how other industries market has been tremendously useful in trying new ideas in dental.

A born and raised New York City Girl, I now call the East End of Long Island home. I get to share it with my amazing husband, a former firefighter (now writer) and our 4-legged kids, CJ and Coco—the original WorkingCat.

I founded WorkingCat Marketing out of a desire to fill a gap I saw in so many practices. Marketing is often the last thing a practice thinks about when it should really be part of your opening checklist. At WorkingCat Marketing, we provide private client coaching so teams can learn to manage their on-line image through social media, YouTube, and other outlets. We also offer done-for-you services like branding and logo design, and professional video and photography.

You can learn more about what we do here at www.WorkingCat.pro and follow me on Instagram at @workingcat_inc. I'm on there all the time. I really should be more focused..... 😺